The Poet Li Po

A.D. 701-762

Arthur Waley

And

Bai Li

THE POET LI PO
A.D. 701-762

INTRODUCTION

Since the Middle Ages the Chinese have been almost unanimous in regarding Li Po as their greatest poet, and the few who have given the first place to his contemporary Tu Fu have usually accorded the second to Li.

One is reluctant to disregard the verdict of a people upon its own poets. We are sometimes told by Frenchmen or Russians that Oscar Wilde is greater than Shakespeare. We are tempted to reply that no foreigner can be qualified to decide such a point.

Yet we do not in practice accept the judgment of other nations upon their own literature. To most Germans Schiller is still a great poet; but to the rest of Europe hardly one at all.

It is consoling to discover that on some Germans (Lilienkron, for example) Schiller makes precisely the same impression as he does on us. And similarly, if we cannot accept the current estimate of Li Po, we have at least the satisfaction of knowing that some of China's most celebrated writers are on our side. About A.D. 816 the poet Po Chü-i wrote as follows (he is discussing Tu Fu as well as Li Po): "The world acclaims Li Po as its master poet. I grant that his works show unparalleled talent and originality, but not one in ten contains any moral reflection or deeper meaning.

"Tu Fu's poems are very numerous; perhaps about 1,000 of them are worth preserving. In the art of stringing together allusions ancient and modern and in the skill of his versification in the regular metres he even excels Li Po. But such poems as the 'Pressgang,'[1] and such lines as

"'At the Palace Gate, the smell of wine and meat; Out in the road, one who has frozen to death'

form only a small proportion of his whole work."

The poet Yüan Chēn (779-831) wrote a famous essay comparing Li Po with Tu Fu.

"At this time," he says (*i.e.*, at the time of Tu Fu), "Li Po from Shantung was also celebrated for his remarkable writings, and the names of these two were often coupled together. In my judgment, as regards impassioned vigour of style, freedom from conventional restraint, and skill in the mere description of exterior things, his ballads and songs are certainly worthy to rub shoulders with Fu. But in disposition of the several parts of a poem, in carrying the balance of rhyme and tone through a composition of several hundred or even in some cases of a thousand words, in grandeur of inspiration combined with harmonious rhythm and deep feeling, in emphasis of parallel clauses, in exclusion of the vulgar or modern—in all these qualities Li is not worthy to approach Fu's front hedge, let alone his inner chamber!"

"Subsequent writers," adds the "T'ang History" (the work in which this essay is preserved), "have agreed with Yüan Chēn."

Wang An-shih (1021-1086), the great reformer of the eleventh century, observes: "Li Po's style is swift, yet never careless; lively, yet never informal. But his intellectual outlook was low and sordid. In nine poems out of ten he deals with nothing but wine or women."

In the "Yü Yin Ts'ung Hua," Hu Tzŭ (*circa* 1120) says: "Wang An-shih, in enumerating China's four greatest poets, put Li Po fourth on the list. Many vulgar people expressed surprise, but Wang replied: 'The reason why vulgar people find Li Po's poetry congenial is that it is easy to enjoy. His intellectual outlook was mean and sordid, and out of ten poems nine deal with wine or women; nevertheless, the abundance of his talent makes it impossible to leave him out of account.'"

Finally Huang T'ing-chien (A.D. 1050-1110), accepted by the Chinese as one of their greatest writers, says with reference to Li's poetry: "The quest for unusual expressions is in itself a literary disease. It was, indeed, this fashion which caused the decay which set in after the Chien-an period (*i.e.*, at the beginning of the third century A.D.)."

To these native strictures very little need be added. No one who reads much of Li's poetry in the original can fail to notice the two defects which are emphasized by the Sung critics. The long poems are often ill-constructed. Where, for example, he wishes to convey an impression of horror he is apt to exhaust himself in the first quatrain, and the rest of the poem is a network of straggling repetitions. Very few of these longer poems have been translated. The second defect, his lack of variety, is one which would only strike those who have read a large number of his poems. Translators have naturally made their selections as varied as possible, so that many of those who know the poet only in translation might feel inclined to defend him on this score. According to Wang An-shih, his two subjects are wine and women. The second does not, of course, imply love-poetry, but sentiments put into the mouths of deserted wives and concubines. Such themes are always felt by the Chinese to be in part allegorical, the deserted lady symbolizing the minister whose counsels a wicked monarch will not heed.

Such poems form the dullest section of Chinese poetry, and are certainly frequent in Li's works. But his most monotonous feature is the mechanical recurrence of certain reflections about the impermanence of human things, as opposed to the immutability of Nature. Probably about half the poems contain some reference to the fact that rivers do not return to their sources, while man changes hour by hour.

The obsession of impermanence has often been sublimated into great mystic poetry. In Li Po it results only in endless restatement of obvious facts.

It has, I think, been generally realized that his strength lies not in the content, but in the form of his poetry. Above all, he was a songwriter. Most of the pieces translated previously and most of those I am going to read to-day are songs, not poems. It is noteworthy that his tombstone bore the inscription, "His skill lay in the writing of archaic songs." His immediate predecessors had carried to the highest refinement the art of writing in elaborate patterns of tone. In Li's whole works there are said to be only nine poems in the strict seven-character metre. Most of his familiar short poems are in the old style, which neglects the formal arrangement of tones. The value of his poetry lay in beauty of words, not in beauty of thought. Unfortunately no one either here or in China can appreciate the music of his verse, for we do not know how Chinese was pronounced in the eighth century. Even to the modern Chinese, his poetry exists more for the eye than for the ear.

The last point to which I shall refer is the extreme allusiveness of his poems. This characteristic, common to most Chinese poetry, is carried to an extreme point in the fifty-nine Old Style poems with which the works begin. Not only do they bristle with the names of historical personages, but almost every phrase is borrowed from some classic. One is tempted to quarrel with Wang An-shih's statement that people liked the poems because they were easy to enjoy. No modern could understand them without pages of commentary to each poem. But Chinese poetry, with a few exceptions, has been written on this principle since the Han dynasty; one poet alone, Po Chü-i, broke through the restraints of pedantry, erasing every expression that his charwoman could not understand.

Translators have naturally avoided the most allusive poems and have omitted or generalized such allusions as occurred. They have frequently failed to recognize allusions as such, and have mistranslated them accordingly, often turning proper names into romantic sentiments.

Li's reputation, like all success, is due partly to accident. After suffering a temporary eclipse during the Sung dynasty, he came back into favour in the sixteenth century, when most of the popular anthologies were made. These compilations devote an inordinate space to his works, and he has been held in corresponding esteem by a public whose knowledge of poetry is chiefly confined to anthologies.

Serious literary criticism has been dead in China since that time, and the valuations then made are still accepted.

Like Miss Havisham's clock, which stopped at twenty to nine on her wedding-day, the clock of Chinese esteem stopped at Li Po centuries ago, and has stuck there ever since.

But I venture to surmise that if a dozen representative English poets could read Chinese poetry in the original, they would none of them give either the first or second place to Li Po.

XXXI. 25.

LIFE OF LI PO, FROM THE "NEW HISTORY OF THE T'ANG DYNASTY," COMPOSED IN THE ELEVENTH CENTURY.

Li Po, styled T'ai-po, was descended in the ninth generation from the Emperor Hsing-shēng.[2] One of his ancestors was charged with a crime at the end of the Sui dynasty,[3] and took refuge in Turkestan.

At the beginning of the period Shēn-lung[4] the family returned and settled in Pa-hsi.[5] At his birth Po's mother dreamt of the planet Ch'ang-kēng [Venus], and that was why he was called Po.[6]

At ten he had mastered the Book of Odes and Book of History. When he grew up he retired to the Min Mountains, and even when summoned to the provincial examinations he made no response. When Su T'ing[7] became Governor of I-chou, he was introduced to Po, and was astonished by him, remarking: "This man has conspicuous natural talents. If he had more learning he would be a second Ssŭ-ma Hsiang-ju."[8] However, he was interested in politics and fond of fencing, becoming one of those knight-errants who care nothing for wealth and much for almsgiving.

Once he stayed at Jēn-ch'ēng[9] with K'ung Ch'ao-fu, Han Chun, P'ei Chēng, Chang Shu-ming, and T'ao Mien. They lived on Mount Ch'u Lai, and were dead drunk every day. People called them the Six Hermits of the Bamboo Stream.

At the beginning of the T'ien-pao period[10] he went south to Kuei-chi, and became intimate with Wu Yün. Wu Yün was summoned by the Emperor, and Po went with him to Ch'ang-an. Here he visited Ho Chih-chang. When Chih-chang read some of his work, he sighed and said: "You are an exiled fairy." He told the Emperor, who sent for Po and gave him audience in the Golden Bells Hall. The poet submitted an essay dealing with current events. The Emperor bestowed food upon him and stirred the soup with his own hand. He ordered that he should be unofficially attached to the Han Lin Academy, but Po went on drinking in the market-place with his boon-companions.

Once when the Emperor was sitting in the Pavilion of Aloes Wood, he had a sudden stirring of heart, and wanted Po to write a song expressive of his mood. When Po entered in obedience to the summons, he was so drunk that the courtiers were obliged to dab his face with water. When he had recovered a little, he seized a brush and without any effort wrote a composition of flawless grace.

The Emperor was so pleased with Po's talent that whenever he was feasting or drinking he always had this poet to wait upon him. Once when Po was drunk the Emperor ordered [the eunuch] Kao Li-shih to take off Po's shoes. Li-shih, who thought such a task beneath him, took revenge by affecting to discover in one of Po's poems a veiled attack on [the Emperor's mistress] Yang Kuei-fei.

Whenever the Emperor thought of giving the poet some official rank, Kuei-fei intervened and dissuaded him.

Po himself, soon realizing that he was unsuited to Court life, allowed his conduct to become more and more reckless and unrestrained.

Together with his friends Ho Chih-chang, Li Shih-chih, Chin, Prince of Ju-yang, Ts'ui Tsung-chih, Su Chin, Chang Hsü, and Chiao Sui, he formed the association known as the Eight Immortals of the Winecup.

He begged persistently to be allowed to retire from Court. At last the Emperor gave him gold and sent him away. Po roamed the country in every direction. Once he went by boat with Ts'ui Tsung-chih from Pien-shih to Nanking. He wore his embroidered Court cloak and sat as proudly in the boat as though he were king of the universe.

When the An Lu-shan revolution broke out, he took to living sometimes at Su-sung, sometimes on Mount K'uang-lu.

Lin, Prince of Yung, gave him the post of assistant on his staff. When Lin took up arms, he fled to P'ēng-tsē. When Lin was defeated, Po was condemned to death. When Po first visited T'ai-yüan Fu, he had seen and admired Kuo Tzŭ-i.[11] On one occasion, when Tzŭ-i was accused of breaking the law, Li Po had come to his assistance and had him released.

Now, hearing of Po's predicament, Tzŭ-i threatened to resign unless Po were saved. The Emperor remitted the sentence of death and changed it to one of perpetual exile at Yeh-lang.[12] But when the amnesty was declared he came back to Kiukiang. Here he was put on trial and sent to gaol. But it happened that Sung Jo-ssŭ was marching to Honan with three thousand soldiers from Kiangsu. He passed through Kiukiang on his way, and released the prisoners there. He gave Li Po an appointment on his staff. Po soon resigned.

When Li Yang-ping became Governor of T'ang-tu, Po went to live near him.

The Emperor Tai Tsung[13] wished to raise him to the rank of Senior Reviser. But when the order came Po was already dead, having reached the age of somewhat over sixty. His last years were devoted to the study of Taoism.

He once crossed the Bull Island Eddies and, reaching Ku-shu, was delighted by a place called the Green Hill, which lay in the estate of the Hsieh family. He expressed a desire to be buried there, but when he died they buried him at Tung-lin.

At the end of the period Yüan-ho,[14] Fan Ch'uan-chēng, Governor of the districts Hsüan and Shē [in Anhui], poured a libation on his grave and forbade the woodmen to cut down the trees which grew there.

He sought for Li Po's descendants, but could only find two granddaughters, who had both married common peasants, but still retained an air of good breeding. They appeared before the Governor weeping, and said: "Our grandfather's wish was to be buried on top of the Green Hill. But they made his grave at the eastern hill-base, which is not what he desired."

Fan Ch'uan-chēng had the grave moved and set up two tombstones. He told the ladies they might change their husbands and marry into the official classes, but they refused, saying that they were pledged to isolation and poverty and could not marry again. Fan was so moved by their reply that he exempted their husbands from national service. A rescript of the Emperor Wēn Tsung created the category of the

Three Paragons: Li Po, of poetry; P'ei Min, of swordsmanship; and Chang Hsü, of cursive calligraphy.

Most of the accounts of Li Po's life which have hitherto appeared are based on the biography given in vol. v. of the "Mémoires Concernant Les Chinois." It is evident that several of the frequently quoted anecdotes in the "Mémoires" are partly based on a misunderstanding of the Chinese text, partly due to the lively imagination of the Jesuits. The Sung writer Hsieh Chung-yung arranged in chronological order all the information about the poet's life that can be gleaned not only from the T'ang histories, but also from the poems themselves.

In the communications of the Gesellschaft für Natur und Völkerkunde, 1889, Dr. Florenz makes some rather haphazard and inaccurate selections from this chronology.

The Life in the "New T'ang History" has, I believe, never before been translated in full. The Life in the so-called "Old T'ang History" is shorter and contains several mistakes. Thus Li is said to have been a native of the Province Shantung, which is certainly untrue.

The following additional facts are based on statements in the poet's own works.

With regard to his marriage in A.D. 730 he writes to a friend: "The land of Ch'u has seven swamps; I went to look at them. But at His Excellency Hsü's house I was offered the hand of his grand-daughter, and lingered there during the frosts of three autumns." He then seems to have abandoned Miss Hsü, who was impatient at his lack of promotion. He afterwards married successively Miss Lin, Miss Lu, and Miss Sung. These were, of course, wives, not concubines. We are told that he was fond of "going about with the dancing-girls of Chao-yang and Chin-ling." He had one son, who died in A.D. 797.

With regard to his part in the revolution, the "New History" seems somewhat confused. It is probable that his sojourn in the prison at

Kiukiang took place before and not after his decree of banishment. It is also uncertain whether he knew, when he entered the service of Lin, that this prince was about to take up arms against the Emperor. The Chinese have reproached Po with ingratitude to his Imperial patron, but it would appear that he abandoned Prince Lin as soon as the latter joined the revolution.

A mysterious figure mentioned in the poems is the "High Priest of Pei-hai" [in Shantung], from whom the poet received a diploma of Taoist proficiency in A.D. 746.

Li Yang-ping gives the following account of Po's death: "When he was about to hang up his cap [an euphemism for "dying"] Li Po was worried at the thought that his numerous rough drafts had not been collected and arranged. Lying on his pillow, he gave over to me all his documents, that I might put them in order."

The "Old T'ang History" says that his illness was due to excessive drinking. There is nothing improbable in the diagnosis. There is a legend[15] that he was drowned while making a drunken effort to embrace the reflection of the moon in the water. This account of his end has been adopted by Giles and most other European writers, but already in the twelfth century Hung Mai pointed out that the story is inconsistent with Li Yang-ping's authentic evidence.

The truth may be that he contracted his last illness as the result of falling into the water while drunk.

THE TEXT OF THE POEMS.

The first edition of the poems was in ten *chüan*, and was published by Li Yang-ping in the year of the poet's death. The preface tells us that Li Po had lost his own MSS. of almost all the poems written during the eight years of his wanderings—that is, from about 753 to 761. A few copies had been procured from friends. About 770 Wei Hao produced an edition of twenty *chüan*, many additional poems having come to light in the interval.

In 998 Yo Shih added the prose works, consisting of five letters and various prefaces, petitions, monumental inscriptions, etc.

In 1080 Sung Min-ch'iu published the works in thirty *chüan*, the form in which they still exist. There are just under 1,000 poems and about sixty prose pieces.

In 1759 an annotated edition was published by Wang Ch'i, with six *chüan* of critical and biographical matter added to the thirty *chüan* of the works.

It is this edition which has been chiefly used by European readers and to which references are made in the present paper. It was reprinted by the Sao Yeh Co. of Shanghai in 1908.

The text of the poems is remarkable for the number of variant readings, which in some cases affect crucial words in quite short poems, in others extend to a whole line or couplet. A printed text of the thirteenth century containing the annotations of Yang Tzŭ-chien is generally followed in current editions. This is known as the Hsiao text; a Ming reprint of it is sometimes met with.

At the beginning of the eighteenth century, a Sung printed edition came into the hands of a Mr. Miu at Soochow; he reprinted it in facsimile. This is known as the Miu text. As there is no means of deciding which of these two has the better authority, my choice of readings has been guided by personal preference.

TRANSLATIONS

II. 7. Ku Fēng, No. 6

The T'ai horse cannot think of Yüeh; The birds of Yüeh have no love for Yen. Feeling and character grow out of habit; A people's customs cannot be changed. Once we marched from the Wild Goose Gate; Now we are fighting in front of the Dragon Pen. Startled sands blur the desert sun;

Flying snows bewilder the Tartar sky. Lice swarm in our plumed caps and tiger coats; Our spirits tremble like the flags we raise to the wind. Hard fighting gets no reward or praise; Steadfastness and truth cannot be rightly known. Who was sorry for Li, the Swift of Wing,[16] When his white head vanished from the Three Fronts?[17]

III. 1. The Distant Parting

Long ago there were two queens[18] called Huang and Ying. And they stood on the shores of the Hsiao-hsiang, to the south of Lake Tung-t'ing. Their sorrow was deep as the waters of the Lake that go straight down a thousand miles. Dark clouds blackened the sun. Shōjō[19] howled in the mist and ghosts whistled in the rain. The queens said, "Though we speak of it we cannot mend it. High Heaven is secretly afraid to shine on our loyalty. But the thunder crashes and bellows its anger, that while Yao and Shun are here they should also be crowning Yü. When a prince loses his servants, the dragon turns into a minnow. When power goes to slaves, mice change to tigers.

"Some say that Yao is shackled and hidden away, and that Shun has died in the fields.

"But the Nine Hills of Deceit stand there in a row, each like each; and which of them covers the lonely bones of the Double-eyed One, our Master?"

So the royal ladies wept, standing amid yellow clouds. Their tears followed the winds and waves, that never return. And while they wept, they looked out into the distance and saw the deep mountain of Tsang-wu.

"The mountain of Tsang-wu shall fall and the waters of the Hsiang shall cease, sooner than the marks of our tears shall fade from these bamboo-leaves."

[Of this poem and the "Szechwan Road" a critic has said: "You could recite them all day without growing tired of them."]

III. 4. The Szechwan Road

Eheu! How dangerous, how high! It would be easier to climb to Heaven than to walk the Szechwan Road.

Since Ts'an Ts'ung and Yü Fu ruled the land, forty-eight thousand years had gone by; and still no human foot had passed from Shu to the frontiers of Ch'in. To the west across T'ai-po Shan there was a bird-track, by which one could cross to the ridge of O-mi. But the earth of the hill crumbled and heroes[20] perished.

So afterwards they made sky ladders and hanging bridges. Above, high beacons of rock that turn back the chariot of the sun. Below, whirling eddies that meet the waves of the current and drive them away. Even the wings of the yellow cranes cannot carry them across, and the monkeys grow weary of such climbing.

How the road curls in the pass of Green Mud!

With nine turns in a hundred steps it twists up the hills.

Clutching at Orion, passing the Well Star, I look up and gasp. Then beating my breast sit and groan aloud.

I fear I shall never return from my westward wandering; the way is steep and the rocks cannot be climbed.

Sometimes the voice of a bird calls among the ancient trees—a male calling to its wife, up and down through the woods. Sometimes a nightingale sings to the moon, weary of empty hills.

It would be easier to climb to Heaven than to walk the Szechwan Road; and those who hear the tale of it turn pale with fear.

Between the hill-tops and the sky there is not a cubit's space. Withered pine-trees hang leaning over precipitous walls.

Flying waterfalls and rolling torrents mingle their din. Beating the cliffs and circling the rocks, they thunder in a thousand valleys.

Alas! O traveller, why did you come to so fearful a place? The Sword Gate is high and jagged. If one man stood in the Pass, he could hold it against ten thousand.

The guardian of the Pass leaps like a wolf on all who are not his kinsmen.

In the daytime one hides from ravening tigers and in the night from long serpents, that sharpen their fangs and lick blood, slaying men like grass.

They say the Embroidered City is a pleasant place, but I had rather be safe at home.

For it would be easier to climb to Heaven than to walk the Szechwan Road.

I turn my body and gaze longingly towards the West.

[When Li Po came to the capital and showed this poem to Ho Chih-ch'ang, Chih-ch'ang raised his eyebrows and said: "Sir, you are not a man of this world. You must indeed be the genius of the star T'ai-po" (xxxiv. 36).]

III. 15. Fighting

Last year we were fighting at the source of the San-kan; This year we are fighting at the Onion River road. We have washed our swords in the surf of Indian seas; We have pastured our horses among the snows of T'ien Shan. Three armies have grown gray and old, Fighting ten thousand leagues away from home. The Huns have no trade but battle and carnage; They have no pastures or ploughlands, But only wastes where white bones lie among yellow sands. Where the house of Ch'in built the great wall that was to keep away the Tartars, There, in its turn, the house of Han lit beacons of war. The beacons are always alight; fighting and marching never stop. Men die in the field, slashing sword to sword; The horses of the conquered neigh piteously to Heaven. Crows and hawks peck for human guts, Carry them in their beaks and hang them on the branches of withered trees. Captains and soldiers are smeared on the bushes and grass; The General schemed in vain. Know therefore that the sword is a cursèd thing Which the wise man uses only if he must.

III. 16. Drinking Song

See the waters of the Yellow River leap down from Heaven, Roll away to the deep sea and never turn again! See at the mirror in the High Hall Aged men bewailing white locks— In the morning, threads of silk; In the evening flakes of snow! Snatch the joys of life as they come and use them to the fill; Do not leave the silver cup idly glinting at the moon. The things Heaven made Man was meant to use; A thousand guilders scattered to the wind may come back again. Roast mutton and sliced beef will only taste well If you drink with them at one sitting three hundred cups. Master Ts'ēn Ts'an, Doctor Tan-ch'iu, Here is wine: do not stop drinking, But listen, please, and I will sing you a song.

Bells and drums and fine food, what are *they* to me, Who only want to get drunk and never again be sober? The Saints and Sages of old times are all stock and still; Only the mighty drinkers of wine have left a name behind. When the king of Ch'ēn gave a feast in the Palace of P'ing-lo With twenty thousand gallons of wine he loosed mirth and play. The master of the feast must not cry that his money is all spent; Let him send to the tavern and fetch more, to keep your glasses filled. His five-flower horse and thousand-guilder coat— Let him call his boy to take them along and sell them for good wine, That drinking together we may drive away the sorrows of a thousand years.

III. 26. The Sun

O Sun that rose in the eastern corner of Earth, Looking as though you came from under the ground, When you crossed the sky and entered the deep sea, Where did you stable your six dragon-steeds? Now and of old your journeys have never ceased: Strong were that man's limbs Who could run beside you on your travels to and fro.

The grass does not refuse To flourish in the spring wind; The leaves are not angry At falling through the autumn sky. Who with whip or spur Can urge the feet of Time? The things of the world flourish and decay, Each at its own hour.

Hsi-ho, Hsi-ho,[21] Is it true that once you loitered in the West While Lu Yang[22] raised his spear, to hold The progress of your light; Then plunged and sank in the turmoil of the sea? Rebels against Heaven, slanderers of Fate; Many defy the Way. But / will put | the Whole Lump | of Life in my bag, And merge my being in the Primal Element.

IV. 19. On the Banks of Jo-yeh

By the river-side at Jo-yeh, girls plucking lotus; Laughing across the lotus-flowers, each whispers to a friend. Their powdered cheeks, lit by the sun, are mirrored deep in the pool; Their scented skirts, caught by the wind, flap high in the air.

Who are these gaily riding along the river-bank, Three by three and five by five, glinting through the willow-boughs? Deep the hoofs of their neighing roans sink into the fallen leaves; The riders see, for a moment pause, and are gone with a pang at heart.

IV. 24. Ch'ang-kan

Soon after I wore my hair covering my forehead I was plucking flowers and playing in front of the gate, When *you* came by, walking on bamboo-stilts Along the trellis,[23] playing with the green plums. We both lived in the village of Ch'ang-kan, Two children, without hate or suspicion. At fourteen I became your wife; I was shame-faced and never dared smile. I sank my head against the dark wall; Called to a thousand times, I did not turn. At fifteen I stopped wrinkling my brow And desired my ashes to be mingled with your dust. I thought you were like the man who clung to the bridge:[24] Not guessing I should climb the Look-for-Husband Terrace,[25] But next year you went far away, To Ch'ü-t'ang and the Whirling Water Rocks. In the fifth month "one should not venture there"[26] Where wailing monkeys cluster in the cliffs above. In front of the door, the tracks you once made One by one have been covered by green moss— Moss so thick that I cannot sweep it away, And leaves are falling in the early autumn wind. Yellow with August the pairing butterflies In the western garden flit from grass to grass. The sight of these wounds my heart with pain; As I sit and sorrow, my red cheeks fade. Send me a letter and let me know in time When your boat will be going through the three gorges of Pa. I will come to meet you as far as ever you please, Even to the dangerous sands of Ch'ang-fēng.

VII. 4. River Song

Of satin-wood our boat is made, Our oars of ebony;[27] Jade pipes and gold flutes Play at stern and prow. A thousand gallons of red wine We carry in the ship's hold; With girls on board at the waves' will We are glad to drift or stay. Even the rishi[28] had to wait For a yellow crane to ride; But the sailor[29] whose heart had no guile Was followed by the white gulls. Ch'ü P'ing's[30] prose and verse Hang like the sun and moon;[31] The king of Ch'u's arbours and towers Are only hummocks in the ground. With my mood at its height I wield my brush And the Five Hills quake;

When the poem is done, my laughter soars To the Blue Isles[32] of the sky. Riches, Honour, Triumph, Fame, Than that *you* should long endure, It were likelier the stream of the River Han Should flow to the North-West!

XIII. 11. Sent to the Commissary Yüan of Ch'iao City, in Memory of Former Excursions

Do you remember how once at Lo-yang, Tung Tsao-ch'in built us a wine-tower south of the T'ien-ching Bridge?

With yellow gold and tallies of white jade we bought songs and laughter, and we were drunk month after month, with no thought of kings and princes, though among us were the wisest and bravest within the Four Seas, and men of high promotion.[33]

(But with you above all my heart was at no cross-purpose.)[34] Going round mountains and skirting lakes was as nothing to them. They poured out their hearts and minds, and held nothing back.

Then I went off to Huai-nan to pluck the laurel-branches,[35] and you stayed north of the Lo, sighing over thoughts and dreams.

We could not endure separation. We sought each other out and went on and on together, exploring the Fairy Castle.[36]

We followed the thirty-six bends of the twisting waters, and all along the streams a thousand different flowers were in bloom. We passed through ten thousand valleys, and in each we heard the voice of wind among the pines.

Then the Governor of Han-tung came out to meet us, on a silver saddle with tassels of gold that reached to the ground. And the Initiate of Tzŭ-yang[37] summoned us, blowing on his jade *shēng*. And Sennin music was made in the tower of Ts'an Hsia,[38] loud as the blended voices of phœnix and roc.

And the Governor of Han-tung, because his long sleeves would not keep still when the flutes called to him, rose and drunkenly danced. Then he brought his embroidered coat and covered me with it, and I slept with my head on his lap.

At the feast our spirits had soared to the Nine Heavens, but before evening we were scattered like stars or rain, flying away over hills and rivers to the frontier of Ch'u. I went back to my mountain to seek my old nest, and you, too, went home, crossing the Wei Bridge.

Then your father, who was brave as leopard or tiger, became Governor of Ping-chou[39] and put down the rebel bands. And in the fifth month he sent for me. I crossed the T'ai-hang Mountains; and though it was hard going on the Sheep's Gut Hills, I paid no heed to broken wheels.

When at last, far on into Winter, I got to the Northern Capital,[40] I was moved to see how much you cared for my reception and how little you cared for the cost—amber cups and fine foods on a blue jade dish. You made me drunk and satisfied. I had no thought of returning.

Sometimes we went out towards the western corner of the City, to where waters like green jade flow round the temple of Shu Yü.[41] We launched our boat and sported on the stream, while flutes and drums sounded. The little waves were like dragon-scales, and the sedge-leaves were pale green. When it was our mood, we took girls with us and gave ourselves to the moments that passed, forgetting that it would soon be over, like willow-flowers or snow. Rouged faces, flushed with drink, looked well in the sunset. Clear water a hundred feet deep reflected the faces of the singers—singing-girls delicate and graceful in the light of the young moon. And the girls sang again and again to make the gauze dresses dance. The clear wind blew the songs away into the empty sky: the sound coiled in the air like moving clouds in flight.

The pleasures of those times shall never again be met with. I went West to offer up a Ballad of Tall Willows,[42] but got no promotion at the Northern Gate and, white-headed, went back to the Eastern Hills.

Once we met at the Southern end of Wei Bridge, but scattered again to the north of the Tso Terrace.

And if you ask me how many are my regrets at this parting, I will tell you they come from me thick as the flowers that fall at Spring's end.

But I cannot tell you all I feel; I could not even if I went on talking for ever. So I call in the boy and make him kneel here and tie this up, and send it to you, a remembrance, from a thousand miles away.

XV. 2. A Dream of T'ien-mu Mountain

(Part of a Poem in Irregular Metre.)

On through the night I flew, high over the Mirror Lake. The lake-moon cast my shadow on the waves and travelled with me to the stream of Shan. The Lord Hsieh's[43] lodging-place was still there. The blue waters rippled; the cry of the apes was shrill. I shod my feet with the shoes of the Lord Hsieh and "climbed to Heaven on a ladder of dark clouds."[44] Half-way up, I saw the unrisen sun hiding behind the sea and heard the Cock of Heaven crowing in the sky. By a thousand broken paths I twisted and turned from crag to crag. My eyes grew dim. I clutched at the rocks, and all was dark.

The roaring of bears and the singing of dragons echoed amid the stones and streams. The darkness of deep woods made me afraid. I trembled at the storied cliffs.

The clouds hung dark, as though they would rain; the air was dim with the spray of rushing waters.

Lightning flashed: thunder roared. Peaks and ridges tottered and broke. Suddenly the walls of the hollow where I stood sundered with a crash, and I looked down on a bottomless void of blue, where the sun and moon gleamed on a terrace of silver and gold.

A host of Beings descended—Cloud-spirits, whose coats were made of rainbow and the horses they rode on were the winds.

XV. 16. Parting with Friends at a Wineshop in Nanking

The wind blowing through the willow-flowers fills the shop with scent; A girl of Wu has served wine and bids the traveller taste. The young men of Nanking have come to see me off; I that go and you that stay | must each drink his cup. I beg you tell the Great River | whose stream flows to the East That thoughts of you will cling to my heart | when *he* has ceased to flow.

XV. 28. At Chiang-hsia, parting from Sung Chih-t'i

Clear as the sky the waters of Hupeh Far away will join with the Blue Sea; We whom a thousand miles will soon part Can mend our grief only with a cup of wine. The valley birds are singing in the bright sun; The river monkeys wail down the evening wind. And I, who in all my life have seldom wept, Am weeping now with tears that will never dry.

XX. 1. The White River at Nan-yang

Wading at dawn the White River's source, Severed a while from the common ways of men, To islands tinged with the colours of Paradise, Where the river sky drowns in limpid space. While my eyes were watching the clouds that travel to the sea. My heart was idle as the fish that swim in the stream. With long singing I put the sun to rest: Riding the moon,[45] came back to my fields and home.

XX. 1. The Clear Cold Spring

(*Literal Version.*)

Regret that dropping sun's dusk; Love this cold stream's clearness. Western beams follow flowing water; Stir a ripple in wandering person's mind. Idly sing, gazing at cloudy moon; Song done—sound of tall pines.

XX. 8. Going down Chung-nan Mountain and spending the Night drinking with the Hermit Tou-ssŭ

At dusk we left the blue mountain-head; The mountain-moon followed our homeward steps. We looked round: the path by which we had come Was a dark cleft across the shoulder of the hill. Hand in hand we reached the walls of the farm; A young boy opened the wicker-gate. Through green bamboos a deep road ran Where dark creepers brushed our coats as we passed. We were glad at last to come to a place of rest, With wine enough to drink together to our fill, Long I sang to the tune of the Pine-tree Wind; When the song was over, the River-stars[46] were few. *I* was drunk and you happy at my side; Till mingled joy drove the World from our hearts.

XXIII. 3. Drinking alone by Moonlight

(1)

A cup of wine, under the flowering-trees: I drink alone, for no friend is near. Raising my cup, I beckon the bright moon, For he, with my shadow, will make three men. The moon, alas! is no drinker of wine: Listless, my shadow creeps about at my side. Yet with the moon as friend and the shadow as slave I must make merry before the Spring is spent. To the songs I sing the moon flickers her beams; In the dance I weave my shadow tangles and breaks. While we were sober, three shared the fun; Now we are drunk, each goes his way. May we long share our odd, inanimate feast, And meet at last on the Cloudy River of the Sky.[47]

(2)

In the third month the town of Hsien-yang Is thick-spread with a carpet of fallen flowers. Who in Spring can bear to grieve alone? Who, sober, look on sights like these? Riches and Poverty, long or short life, By the Maker of Things are portioned and disposed. But a cup of wine levels life and death And a thousand things obstinately hard to prove. When I am drunk, I lose Heaven and Earth; Motionless, I cleave to my lonely bed. At last I forget that I exist at all, And at *that* moment my joy is great indeed.

(3)

If High Heaven had no love for wine, There would not be a Wine Star in the sky. If Earth herself had no love for wine, There would not be a city called Wine Springs.[48] Since Heaven and Earth both love wine, I can love wine, without shame before God. Clear wine was once called "a Saint;" Thick wine was once called "a Sage."[49] Of Saint and Sage I have long quaffed deep, What need for me to study spirits and *hsien*?[50] At the third cup I penetrate the Great Way; A full gallon—Nature and I are one.... But the things I feel when wine possesses my soul I will never tell to those who are not drunk.

XXIII. 9. In the Mountains on a Summer Day

Gently I stir a white feather fan, With open shirt, sitting in a green wood. I take off my cap and hang it on a jutting stone: A wind from the pine-trees trickles on my bare head.

XXIII. 10. Drinking together in the Mountains

Two men drinking together where mountain flowers grow: One cup, one cup, and again one cup. "Now I am drunk and would like to sleep: so please go away. Come back to-morrow, if you feel inclined, and bring your harp with you."

XXIII. 10. Waking from Drunkenness on a Spring Day

"Life in the World is but a big dream: I will not spoil it by any labour or care." So saying, I was drunk all the day, Lying helpless at the porch in front of my door. When I woke up, I blinked at the garden lawn; A lonely bird was singing amid the flowers. I asked myself, had the day been wet or fine? The Spring wind was telling the mango-bird. Moved by its song, I soon began to sigh, And as wine was there, I filled my own cup. Wildly singing, I waited for the moon to rise, When my song was over, all my senses had gone.

XXIII. 13. Self-Abandonment

I sat drinking and did not notice the dusk, Till falling petals filled the folds of my dress. Drunken I rose and walked to the moonlit stream; The birds were gone, and men also few.

XXV. 1. To Tan Ch'iu

My friend is lodging high in the Eastern Range, Dearly loving the beauty of valleys and hills. At Green Spring he lies in the empty woods; And is still asleep when the sun shines on high. A pine-tree wind dusts his sleeves and coat; A pebbly stream cleans his heart and ears. I envy you, who far from strife and talk Are high-propped on a pillow of blue cloud.

XXX. 8. Clearing up at Dawn

The fields are chill; the sparse rain has stopped; The colours of Spring teem on every side. With leaping fish the blue pond is full; With singing thrushes the green boughs droop. The flowers of the field have dabbled their powdered cheeks; The mountain grasses are bent level at the waist. By the bamboo stream the last fragments of cloud Blown by the wind slowly scatter away.

[Many of the above poems have been translated before, in some cases by three or four different hands. But , , , and are, so far as I know, translated for the first time.]

DISCUSSION ON THE FOREGOING PAPER

The Chairman (Mr. George Jamieson): Mr. Li T'ai-po was, I am afraid, a bit of a Bohemian (laughter), and his Bacchanalian experiences have been repeated in later days even with the great poets. I am sure you will all join with me in expressing a hearty vote of thanks to Mr. Waley for his address and the very felicitous language in which he has translated a number of these ancient poems. I trust his paper will be printed and preserved with the rest of our publications, because these poems, as far as I can judge—but hearing them read does not impress one so much as reading them at leisure—are well worthy of careful perusal. It is curious to note how unchangeable and immobile China is. At the time these poems were written we in Great Britain were living under King Alfred and trying to keep out the Danes and other things. (Laughter.) I can tell you that the Szechwan Road as described in the poem that Mr. Waley has read is just the same now as it was when the poem was written. And the social conditions of the people are the same now as they were at that time. I have often thought that Chinese poets are very limited in their range. They seem to be deficient in the quality of imagination. China has never produced a great epic poem. Of course I speak subject to correction, but I believe I am right in saying that China has never produced a poet comparable with Homer, Dante, Virgil, or Milton. There has been no one born with the power of telling a story like Homer. The poets of China appear to me to be emotional and descriptive, but incapable of any high flights of imagination. I think that Macaulay says that great flights of imagination are peculiar to the early periods of a nation's civilization, and that story-telling reaches its highest form as an art before printing has been much in vogue.

Mr. M. F. A. Fraser: I have listened to this lecture with the greatest interest. The English was particularly pleasing, and I am glad that the lecturer has broken away from the old custom of seeking rhymes, and followed the French custom in the translation of these poems. A man may be an excellent writer and translator, and not be a poet, but to translate foreign poetry into English considerable literary gifts are required.

Mr. Paul King: All of you who have been lately in China must be struck with the extraordinary difference between the China described in these poems and the China which has come into being since the revolution. Ideas of a very practical nature have now taken possession of the people. And then, what about modern Chinese poets? Do any of us know of any? In my intercourse with the Chinese I cannot recall a modern Chinese who was a poet. It is possible that I may have met one, and that he concealed his poetic gifts. (Laughter.) Our lecturer tells us, however, that he knows certain Chinese poets. It would be interesting to know if they are publishing their poems, and how they would compare with the work of the older poets in our possession.

Mr. L. Y. Chen: I should like to join in congratulating Mr. Waley on his very learned paper and beautiful translations. It is quite true that there are no epic poems in Chinese literature. This form of poetry has not been introduced in China, but I differ with your statement, Sir, that Chinese poetry lacks imagination. (Applause.) I could give you many instances to the contrary, though not from memory. The last speaker's remark that the present China is different from what China is in Chinese poetry may be true, but I may well retort that the England as represented in Shakespeare is very different from the England of to-day. (Laughter and cheers.) And Li T'ai-po lived many hundred years ago, but Shakespeare lived at a more recent period. Human nature has two states, the spiritual and the practical. You can combine the two. If you have the practical it does not necessarily follow that you are lacking in the spiritual. As for present-day Chinese poets, there are several famous ones in China.

Since the lecturer has raised the question whether Li T'ai-po or Tu Fu is the greater poet, I would say that the Chinese of the present day consider Tu Fu to be the greater. It strikes me as curious that European people who know something about Chinese poetry should prefer Li T'ai-po. Perhaps very few people have heard of Tu Fu. Certainly there is no translation of the most important of Tu Fu's poems in the English language. In China every child who has studied poetry knows something about Tu Fu's poems. Tu Fu is placed first by the Chinese because he is the greatest national poet. He expresses national feelings in a way that can be appreciated by everybody. Li T'ai-po's poems deal chiefly with wine and women, love and sensual things, but Tu Fu's poems are full of men and women, elderly people and children, their joy, their anguish, the hardship of the soldier, and things of that sort. In a word, Tu Fu's poetry expresses what we ordinary men and women wish to express and cannot.

Mr. G. Willoughby-Meade: One or two observations occur to me in connection with the translation of this poetry into English. The two greatest reading publics are the Anglo-American and the Chinese. The Anglo-American people have produced an enormous amount of poetry which they do not often quote, and the Chinese have produced an enormous amount of poetry which, according to experts, they quote a great deal. Now, at the present moment that peculiar British shyness for quoting poetry seems to have largely disappeared in consequence of the writings of soldier poets. These poems have been written under conditions of great danger, difficulty, and discomfort, and it seems to me that it would be a very good thing if poetry illustrating the thought of these men could be placed before the Anglo-American public.

The Chairman proposed a hearty vote of thanks to the Lecturer, which was carried by acclamation.

FOOTNOTES

[1] Giles, "Chinese Poetry," p. 90.

[2] *I.e.*, Li Kao.

[3] A.D. 581-618.

[4] A.D. 705-707.

[5] In Szechwan.

[6] "Po," "white," was a popular name of the Planet Venus.

[7] Giles, Biog. Dict., No. 1,789.

[8] Giles, No. 1,753.

[9] In Shantung.

[10] *Circa* A.D. 742.

[11] A famous General, the saviour of the dynasty.

[12] In Yunnan.

[13] Reigned 763-780.

[14] 806-821.

[15] The legendary Li Po is the subject of the sixth tale in "Chin Ku Ch'i Kuan", translated by T. Pavie in "Contes et Nouvelles," 1839. He also figures in the Mongol dynasty play, "The Golden Token."

[16] Li Kuang, died 125 B.C.

[17] Manchurian, Mongolian and Turkestan frontiers.

[18] These queens were the daughters of the Emperor Yao, who gave them in marriage to Shun, and abdicated in his favour. Shun's ministers conspired against him and set "the Great Yü" on the throne. A legend says that the spots on the bamboo-leaves which grow on the Hsiang River were caused by the tears of these two queens.

[19] I use the Japanese form as being more familiar. A kind of demon-

monkey is meant.

[20] The "heroes" were five strong men sent by the King of Shu to fetch the five daughters of the King of Ch'in.

[21] Charioteer of the Sun.

[22] Who, like Joshua, stopped the sun during a battle. See Huai-nan Tzǔ, chap. vi.

[23] It is hard to believe that "bed" or "chair" is meant, as hitherto translated. "Trellis" is, however, only a guess.

[24] A man had promised to meet a girl under a bridge. She did not come, but although the water began to rise, he trusted so firmly in her word, that he clung to the pillars of the bridge and waited till he was drowned.

[25] So called because a woman waited there so long for her husband that she turned into stone.

[26] Quotation from the Yangtze boatman's song:

"When Yen-yü is as big as a man's hat One should not venture to make for Ch'ü-t'ang."

[27] A phrase from the Li Sao.

[28] Tou Tzǔ-an, who was carried to Heaven by a yellow crane near Wu-ch'ang.

[29] A story from Lieh Tzu.

[30] *I.e.*, Ch'ü Yüan.

[31] Practically a quotation from Ch'ü Yüan's "Life," by Ssǔ-ma Ch'ien.

[32] Fairyland, sometimes thought of as being in the middle of the sea, sometimes (as here) in the sky.

[33] Lit. "blue clouds people."

[34] A phrase from Chuang Tzŭ.

[35] Huai-nan is associated with laurel-branches, owing to a famous poem by the King of Huai-nan.

[36] Name of a mountain.

[37] *I.e.*, Hu Tzŭ-yang, a Taoist friend of the poet's.

[38] Lit. "Feeding on sunset-cloud" Tower, built by Hu Tzŭ-yang.

[39] *I.e.*, T'ai-yüan Fu.

[40] *I.e.*, T'ai-yüan Fu.

[41] A brother of Prince Ch'ēng, of the Chou dynasty.

[42] Yang Hsiung, died A.D. 18, having lived all his life in obscurity, obtained promotion in his old age by a poem of this title.

[43] Hsieh Ling-yün (*circa* A.D. 400) was a famous mountain-climber who invented special mountain-climbing shoes.

[44] A quotation from one of Hsieh's poems.

[45] *I.e.*, "availing myself of the moonlight."

[46] Stars of the Milky Way.

[47] The Milky Way.

[48] Chiu-ch'üan, in Kansuh.

[49] "History of Wei Dynasty" (Life of Hsü Mo): "A drunken visitor said, 'Clear wine I account a Saint: thick wine only a Sage.'"

[50] Rishi, Immortals.

[51] *Cf. Little Review*, June, 1917, version by Sasaki and M. Bodenheim.

THE END

CPSIA information can be obtained
at www.ICGtesting.com
Printed in the USA
LVHW031107081219
639808LV00003BA/756/P